The Causeway Coastal route begins just outside Larne on the east coast of Northern Ireland, less than 30 miles from Belfast, and winds its way up towards the North Coast, stretching for over 60 miles.

The early part of the route sees a drive along the edge of Ireland with cliffs on one side and the Irish Sea on the other. As you move up the coast the scene becomes yet more dramatic as the stunning Glens of Antrim come to meet the sea at places like Ballygally, Glenarm, Carnlough and Glenariff.

Each stage of the journey gets more breathtaking and the coastline around the small villages of Cushendun and Cushendall is made even more impressive by the steep hills which you encounter on the approach. From here, the proximity to Scotland becomes clear and it looks close enough to touch. Even on a grey autumn day the Mull of Kintyre is clearly visible as the first glimpse of the Scottish coastline.

As we move around the coast past Torr Head we now find ourselves on the north coast of Ireland and we come upon Ballycastle, a picturesque seaside resort town as popular with residents of Northern Ireland as it is for the many international visitors who travel here every year.

Moving on from Ballycastle the cliffs meeting the Atlantic Ocean become even more striking at White Head and White Park Bay before we arrive at the jewel in the Causeway Coast's crown – The Giant's Causeway. Inscribed as a UNESCO World Heritage Site in 1986 the Giant's Causeway is a wonder of nature with over 40,000 polygonal basalt columns rising out of the ocean – the result of an ancient volcanic eruption. This is the number one visitor attraction in Northern Ireland and on arrival here it is easy to see why.

Following the exhilaration of the Giant's Causeway we move on round to the limestone cliffs at Whiterocks beach and the ruins of a medieval fort at Dunluce Castle before coming upon the two seaside resort towns of Portrush and Portstewart. These places need no artificial illuminations as the canvas prepared by nature is enough to leave you in awe. The golden beach at Portstewart Strand stretches on round to Castlerock and Downhill where we are once again greeted by dramatic cliff faces and the Atlantic Ocean – sometimes in angry conflict with each other and sometimes existing together in perfect harmony. Each provides as impressive an image.

From here clear views over to the Inishowen Peninsula can be enjoyed as the dramatic coastline continues into Donegal and beyond, stretching down the West Coast into the counties of Mayo, Sligo, Galway, Clare and Kerry.

People from this part of the world are rightly proud of this mesmerising expanse of coastline. The imagery you encounter on a journey around the Causeway Coast leaves you exhausted as you wait for some respite before the next dramatic episode. The respite never comes and neither would you want it to.

In all four seasons the subject appears so different, yet always breathtaking. When I first visited the area the initial words my local guide spoke to me were 'Welcome to the most beautiful country in the World'. On this evidence it would be hard to disagree.

Rachael Craven

Dunluce Castle – remains of a medieval castle between Portrush and Portballintrae.

The Skerries – a small group of islands visible from many points including Dunluce Castle.

View of the cliffs at Causeway Head taken from Portballintrae.

Portballintrae harbour.

The Old Bushmills Distillery – the world's oldest licensed Whiskey Distillery has been producing Bushmills whiskey since 1608.

The Giant's Causeway & Bushmills Railway Station – links the town of Bushmills and the Giant's Causeway World Heritage Site.

View over to the Mull of Kintyre from White Head.

A church perched on the cliff edge near White Head.

Carrick-a-Rede rope bridge connects Rock Island with the coastal cliffs.

Opposite:
Carrick-a-Rede village looking towards Ballintoy.

Ballintoy harbour – a working harbour for local fishermen.

Opposite:
The beach at White Park Bay with the view continuing to Benbane Head.

Collection of houses and the small harbour near White Park Bay.

A small fishing cottage.

Dunluce Castle ruins with Whiterocks beach and Ramore Head in the background.

The Limestone cliffs of Whiterocks beach on the outskirts of Portrush.

Mussenden Temple at Downhill.

Opposite:
The beach at Downhill with Mussenden Temple
perched on the cliffs in the background.

A view from Magilligan Strand over to Inishowen Head.

A church near Magilligan with Donegal's Inishowen Peninsula in the background.

The Causeway Coastal
Route outside Larne.

A tunnel on the Causeway
Coastal Route with
Ballygally Head visible.

The Four Star Ballygally Castle Hotel, operated by the Hastings Group,
is located at the foot of the Glens of Antrim.

Right:
Birds on the rocks in Drains Bay.

Below:
A familiar sight – sheep in the Glens of Antrim.

Anchor with Ballygalley Head in the background.

Fishing boats in the harbour near Glenarm.

The Glens meet the sea at Glenarm.

Right:
Glendun Viaduct – completed in 1839 – surrounded by the Glens of Antrim.

The village of Cushendun.

The Glens of Antrim from Loughareema looking south.

The River Bann meets the sea at Castlerock.

Opposite:
A view down Portstewart Strand from near Castlerock.

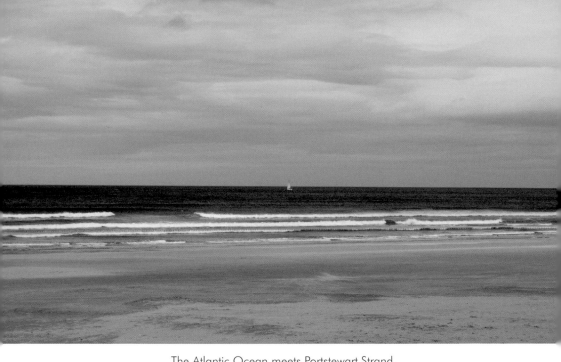

The Atlantic Ocean meets Portstewart Strand.

A ruin on the National Trust-owned Downhill Estate.

The ruins of Downhill House, former home of Frederick Hervey, 4th Earl of Bristol.

A view from the Lion's Gate entrance to Downhill Castle over to Inishowen Head in County Donegal.

A view towards Portstewart and Portrush from Ballyhacket viewing point.

Portrush at dusk.

Opposite:
Portstewart Strand at sunset.

The Portrush Airshow.

The sun sets over the Causeway Coast.

Coastal walk below Portstewart Promenade.

Opposite:
Dominican Convent in Portstewart.

The imposing Glenariff, one of the most famous Glens of Antrim.

Waterfall in Glenariff Forest Park.

The beach at Cushendun.

Garron Point in the background with the village and beach at Cushendun in the foreground.

Opposite:
Fishing boats at Cushendun.

A view over to the Mull of Kintyre from Torr Head.

Torr Head with the Mull of Kintyre across the North Channel.

The Atlantic Ocean meets the shore at Murlough Bay.

Opposite:
Murlough Bay between Ballycastle and Torr Head.

Lough-na-Crannagh near Fair Head.

Rathlin Island – six miles across the Sea of Moyle from Ballycastle.

One of the many small beaches scattered along the Causeway Coast. This one can be found near Corrymeela.

Looking across Ballycastle Bay from Corrymeela.

Maguire's Caravan Site located right on the shore looks across the bay to Rathlin Island.

Fountain on Ballycastle Promenade with the beach in the background.

Opposite:
View from Ballycastle Promenade towards Fair Head.

Boats in the harbour at Ballycastle.

The beach at Ballycastle.

View from the Giant's Causeway Visitor Centre of the walk towards the World Heritage Site.

The Giant's Causeway at the foot of cliffs at Benbane Head.

The pillars of basalt rock that make up the Giant's Causeway.

Opposite:
The Giant's Causeway is an area of about 40,000 interlocking basalt
columns and is the result of an ancient volcanic eruption.

The dramatic cliffs between the Causeway Visitor Centre and the Giant's Causeway.

Close up of the polygonal
columns of layered basalt rock
ul the Giant's Causeway.

A feature in the cliffs near
the Giant's Causeway
known as 'The Piano'.

Green Ireland meets the striking blue sea of the Atlantic Ocean.